ANCIENT MARINE LIFE

MEGALODON

BY KATE MOENING
ILLUSTRATIONS BY MAT EDWARDS

EPIC

BELLWETHER MEDIA • MINNEAPOLIS, MN

EPIC

EPIC BOOKS are no ordinary books. They burst with intense action, high-speed heroics, and shadows of the unknown. Are you ready for an Epic adventure?

This edition first published in 2023 by Bellwether Media, Inc.

No part of this publication may be reproduced in whole or in part without written permission of the publisher. For information regarding permission, write to Bellwether Media, Inc., Attention: Permissions Department, 6012 Blue Circle Drive, Minnetonka, MN 55343.

Library of Congress Cataloging-in-Publication Data

LC record for Megalodon available at: https://lccn.loc.gov/2022050387

Text copyright © 2023 by Bellwether Media, Inc. EPIC and associated logos are trademarks and/or registered trademarks of Bellwether Media, Inc.

Editor: Betsy Rathburn   Designer: Jeffrey Kollock

TABLE OF CONTENTS

WHAT WAS THE MEGALODON?

MAP OF THE WORLD

Neogene period

The megalodon was the biggest shark to ever live!

It first lived around 20 million years ago. This was during the **Neogene period** of the **Cenozoic era**.

The megalodon grew up to 60 feet (18.3 meters) long. It weighed more than 100,000 pounds (45,359 kilograms).

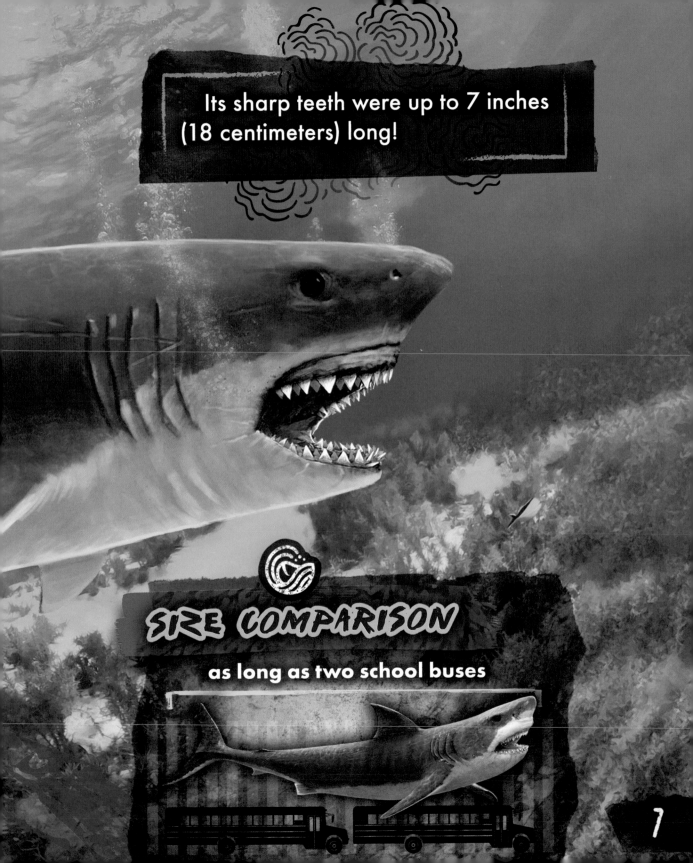

Its sharp teeth were up to 7 inches (18 centimeters) long!

SIZE COMPARISON

as long as two school buses

The megalodon had a strong tail and long fins. These helped it swim fast. Its **skeleton** was made of lightweight **cartilage**. This helped it save **energy**. It could swim far!

fin

A TOOTHY TITLE

The word megalodon comes from Greek. It means "giant tooth!"

tail

THE LIFE OF THE MEGALODON

A MIGHTY BITE

The megalodon was a powerful hunter. Its bite created up to 40,000 pounds (18,144 kilograms) of force!

The megalodon was an **apex predator**. It ate whales, seals, and even other sharks.

The megalodon mostly lived and hunted alone. It ate over 2,000 pounds (907 kilograms) of food every day!

MEGALODON DIET

fish

seals

whales

Adult megalodons had no **predators**. But babies were often hunted.

Females gave birth to live young.
A baby megalodon could be over 6 feet
(1.8 meters) long!

Young megalodons lived with adults in **nurseries**. This helped keep the babies safe.

coral reef nursery

Nurseries were usually in warm, **shallow** water. **Coral reef** nurseries were common. They were full of food!

FOSSILS AND EXTINCTION

The megalodon went **extinct** around 3 million years ago. Ocean **currents** and temperatures were changing.

The changes meant less food for the megalodon. It could not **compete** with other ocean predators.

Cartilage is too soft to make good **fossils**. Most megalodon fossils are teeth.

fossil teeth

ANCIENT MYSTERY

People did not know what the first megalodon fossils were. Many thought that megalodon teeth belonged to dragons!

MEGALODON NURSERY FOSSILS

megalodon fossil

SOUTH AMERICA

FOUND in 2010

LOCATED around Panama

The first were found hundreds of years ago. People still love to study this giant shark!

GET TO KNOW THE MEGALODON

strong tail

LOCATION

around every major landmass except Antarctica

WEIGHT

over 100,000 pounds (45,359 kilograms)

FOOD

whales

seals

fish

SIZE up to 60 feet (18.3 meters) long

Paleozoic

Mesozoic

Cenozoic

Neogene

sharp teeth

cartilage skeleton

FOSSIL FIRST DESCRIBED

in 1835 by Louis Agassiz

GLOSSARY

apex predator—an animal at the top of the food chain that is not preyed upon by other animals

cartilage—a strong but light material that made up the megalodon's skeleton instead of bone

Cenozoic era—a time in history that started 66 million years ago and continues to the present day

compete—to try to get or win something that someone or something else is also trying to get

coral reef—a structure made of coral that usually grows in shallow seawater

currents—patterns of water movement in an ocean

energy—the effort it takes to do something

extinct—no longer living

fossils—remains of living things that lived long ago

Neogene period—a time in history that happened about 23 million to 3 million years ago

nurseries—places where young megalodons were cared for

predators—animals that hunt other animals for food

shallow—not deep

skeleton—the bones or cartilage that support an animal's body

TO LEARN MORE

AT THE LIBRARY

Forster, Miriam. *Sharks!: A Mighty Bite-y History.*
New York, N.Y.: Abrams Books for Young Readers, 2022.

Gagne, Tammy. *Megalodon and Other Prehistoric Sharks.*
North Mankato, Minn.: Capstone Press, 2022.

Zoehfeld, Kathleen Weidner. *Prehistoric: Dinosaurs,*
Megalodons, and Other Fascinating Creatures of the
Deep Past. Greenbelt, Md.: What On Earth Books, 2019.

ON THE WEB

FACTSURFER

Factsurfer.com gives you
a safe, fun way to find
more information.

1. Go to www.factsurfer.com.

2. Enter "megalodon" into the search box
   and click 🔍 .

3. Select your book cover to see a list
   of related content.

INDEX